Distressables & Doo-Dads

Come and join the fun! I really enjoy surprising friends by making tiny works of art with little doo-dads, then sending these Cards in the mail!

My Secret Journey
MATERIALS: Silver bottle cap • Manila mini file folders • Papers: Bingo, Rulers • Cutable doo-dad strips: Letter Squares, Print Blocks • Brown cardstock • 2 small snaps • *Junkitz* Dull Silver D-Ringz • Small Silver brad • *Ranger* Distress ink (Tea Dye, Walnut) • Corner Rounder • Foam tape • Glue stick
INSTRUCTIONS: Cut a $2^{1}/2$" x $3^{1}/2$" piece of Brown cardstock. Cover with Bingo paper and trim. Round corners of card. Age edges of card with Tea Dye.
• Flatten bottle cap. Cut out number from Bingo paper and glue to center. Age edges of mini file folder with Walnut. Slide a strip of foam tape inside folder to prop open slightly. Cut words and letters from cutable doo-dad strips. Age edges with Walnut. Glue to front of folder.
• Cut 2 ruler strips from Rulers paper. Fold one end of each over and slide through d-ring. Stack strips with folds overlapping and brad together. Glue strips to right side of card, trimming to size. Glue snaps to ends of rulers. Glue bottle caps and folder to card.

Life is a Story
MATERIALS: Cutable doo-dad strip: Dark Words • Papers: Journaling, Library • Brown cardstock • Fabric scrap • 2 small Copper brads • *Ranger* Walnut Distress ink • Corner rounder punch • Foam tape • Glue stick
INSTRUCTIONS: Cut a $2^{1}/2$" x $3^{1}/2$" piece of Brown cardstock. Cover with Journaling paper and trim. Round corners of card. Age edges with Walnut. Cut book cover from Library paper. Age edges with Walnut. Attach left side to card with brads. Slide a piece of foam tape under right side to prop up slightly. Cut words from Dark Words strip. Age edges, glue to front of book. Tear a fabric strip and tie on card.

Circus
MATERIALS: Circus paper • Cutable doo-dad strips: Toy Blocks, Typewriter, Print Blocks, Letter Squares • Brown cardstock • *Junkitz* Clearz Four Hole Tilez, Metal Corners • 4 small brads • Rub-on alphabet • Twine • *Ranger* Walnut Distress ink • Corner rounder punch • Glue stick
INSTRUCTIONS: Cut a $2^{1}/2$" x $3^{1}/2$" piece of Brown cardstock. Cover with Circus paper and trim. Round corners of card. Age edges with Walnut. Attach metal corners. Cut ticket from Circus paper and age with Walnut. Punch hole in ticket and tie with twine. Apply rub-on to Clearz. Cut letters from strips and glue to Clearz. Attach Clearz to card with brad. Slip ticket behind Clearz.

Explore Art
MATERIALS: Papers: Time, Rulers, Print Blocks • Cutable doo-dad strips: Letter Squares, Dark Words • Silver metal clip • Brown cardstock • Small key • Stapler • *Junkitz* Silver Metalz Framez • *Ranger* Distress ink (Soot, Walnut) • Corner Rounder punch • Foam tape • Glue stick
INSTRUCTIONS: Cut a $2^{1}/2$" x $3^{1}/2$" piece of Brown cardstock. Cover with Time paper and trim. Round corners of card. Age edges with Walnut. Cut ruler from Rulers paper, and letter from Print Blocks. Age with Soot. Attach ruler to card with staples, and letter with foam tape. Attach clip to letter, and to card with brad. Glue Metalz and key to card. Cut letters and words from strips and age edges. Glue to card.

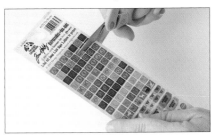

1. Cut or punch Doo-Dad.

2. Sand with sanding block.

3. Age edges with Distress Ink.

I've been making and trading ATCs for quite some time, and my current collection is approaching a thousand cards. Many of the cards included in this book are those I've made for trades and swaps. I hope you enjoy them!

Lisa Vollrath

This information is for an edition of 26 cards. This particular card is number 1 of 26.

Information such as this is for individual cards. This card is the 237th unique card I've made.

What Goes On the Back?

One of the most often asked questions about ATCs is what to put on the back. Each artist approaches this differently, but the basic information you should include is your name, some sort of contact information, and some type of numbering.

About numbering: some artists start with #1 on the very first card they make, and number every card consecutively, in order of completion. Some number cards within an edition or series. Above are some examples of back stickers I've used on my own cards.

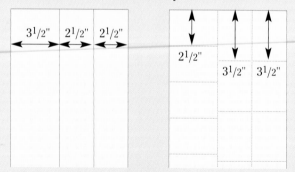

Cutting 10 Cards From One Sheet

I generally make more than one card at a time, so I like to have plenty of blank cards on hand ready to decorate. Here's how to cut 10 cards from one 8$\frac{1}{2}$" x 11" sheet of cardstock with very little waste:

First, cut two lengthwise strips 2$\frac{1}{2}$" wide, leaving one strip 3$\frac{1}{2}$" wide. Then, cut the strips crosswise: the 2$\frac{1}{2}$" strips will be 3$\frac{1}{2}$" wide, and the 3$\frac{1}{2}$" strips will be 2$\frac{1}{2}$" wide. There you have it: 10 cards from one sheet!

Little Star

MATERIALS: Dictionary paper; Coffee Words stickers • $2^1/2$" print of a vintage image • Sage cardstock • Glue stick

INSTRUCTIONS:
Cut a $3^1/2$" x 5" piece from Sage cardstock. Cut a $2^1/4$" x $4^1/2$" piece from Dictionary. Glue to cardstock. Fold in half, then again $1^1/4$" from right side. Cut star shape from vintage image and glue to right side of card. Adhere sticker to inside of card, behind star.

Gazing Geisha

MATERIALS: Ivory cardstock • Asian text paper • 2" x 3" print of geisha photo • Chinese coin • Peace stamp • Black dye ink • Glue stick

INSTRUCTIONS:
Cut a $3^1/2$" x 5" piece of cardstock. Glue Asian text to cardstock. Fold in half. Cut photo in oval shape and glue to left side of card. Mark $1^1/4$" from left side. Cut around right side of oval between marks. Fold card on marks, letting photo pop out to right. Stamp peace on interior of card. Glue the right side of a coin to right side of card to form a closure.

Mona's Treasure

MATERIALS: da Vinci Tiles paper • Ivory parchment cardstock • *Ma Vinci's Reliquary* Mona face stamp • *Melanie Sage* script text stamp • Brown dye ink • *ColorBox* Chestnut Roan chalk inkpad • Glue stick

INSTRUCTIONS:
Cut a $3^1/2$" x 5" piece from cardstock. Fold in half. Stamp Mona face on right side of card. Mark $1^1/4$" from right side. Cut around left side of face between marks. Fold card on marks, letting face pop out to left. Stamp text on left side of card. Age edges with Chestnut Roan inkpad. Cut a square from da Vinci Tiles and glue to inside of card behind face.

Simple Folds

When I first started making ATCs, I felt a little intimidated by the tiny working space. I solved my dilemma by creating cards that magically opened up to reveal extra space.

I still use this design to hide hidden words and special messages.

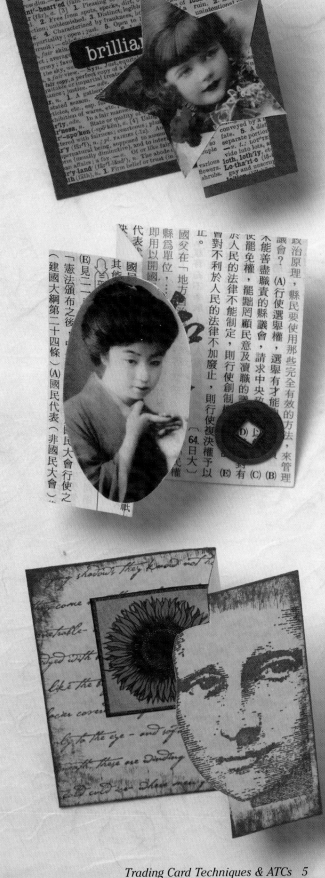

Trading Card Basics

1. Fold a $3^1/2$" x 5" piece of cardstock in half.

2. Stamp image on right side of card.

3. Mark $1^1/4$" from the right edge.

4. Cut around image, starting and ending at marks.

5. Push cut piece outward and fold.

6. Open and decorate the interior.

1. Apply alcohol inks to felt.

2. Pat inks randomly onto surface.

3. Dot card with metallic marker.

4. Apply blending solution to surface with felt.

Polished Stone Finish

This simple technique exploits the quick drying properties of alcohol inks to create a colorful textured background. Apply to glossy paper or anything metal to create lovely watercolor effects.

Cards Keeper

Store finished cards in this lovely metal box.

ATC Box

MATERIALS:
Silver bottle caps • *Ranger* Adirondack inks (Meadow, Slate) • Gold Metallic paint pen • Metal box • Letter stamps • Black dye ink • 1" clear epoxy stickers • E6000 adhesive

INSTRUCTIONS:
Following instructions above, apply alcohol inks to box and bottle caps. When dry, stamp letters on bottle caps. When completely dry, cover caps with clear epoxy stickers and glue to box with E6000.

Geisha Thoughts

MATERIALS:
Dark Words cutable strips • *Ranger* Adirondack inks (Meadow, Slate) • *Krylon* Gold Metallic paint pen • Glossy cardstock • Geisha image • Chinese character stamp • Black dye inkpad • Glue stick

INSTRUCTIONS:
Following steps on page 6, apply alcohol inks to cardstock. Cut a 2 1/2" x 3 1/2" piece from inked cardstock. Cut figure from image and glue to card. Cut word from Doo-Dads strip and glue to card. Stamp character on upper corner.

Juice Lid Joy

MATERIALS:
Tea Dye Script paper • Small Metal Disk • Coffee Words stickers • *Ranger* Adirondack inks (Mushroom, Oregano, Meadow) • *Krylon* Copper Metallic paint pen • Brown cardstock • Striped ribbon • Soda can pull tab • E6000 • Foam tape • Glue stick

INSTRUCTIONS:
Following steps on page 6, apply alcohol inks to juice lid and pull tab. Cut a 2 1/4" x 3 1/4" piece from Tea Dye Script. Wrap ribbon through pull tab. Wrap around Script and glue in place. Cut a 2 1/2" x 3 1/2" piece from cardstock. Glue layers together. Glue juice lid to card. Apply sticker with foam tape.

Vintage Metal

MATERIALS:
Ranger Adirondack inks (Mushroom, Oregano, Meadow) • *Krylon* Copper Metallic paint pen • Transparency • Computer and printer • Metal flashing • Small number stencil • Black permanent marker • Glue stick

INSTRUCTIONS:
Following instructions for metal flashing, cut out card. Following steps on page 6, apply alcohol inks to metal card. Print image on transparency. Cut out around figure and apply to card with glue stick. Apply number to card with stencil and Black marker.

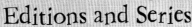

The Rule of '3'

One way to create a clean, uncluttered card is to apply the Rule of 3. Create a card using a background, a focal image, and an embellishment. In the card at right, the background is a piece of cardstock layered with tissue and stamped, the focal point is the figure, and the embellishment is the star.

House of Blues

MATERIALS: Cardstock (Light Blue, Dark Blue) • Rubber stamps (Music, Script, *Stampsmith* MJ Hopper) • Blue tissue • Dye inkpads (Light, Medium and Dark Blue) • Star rhinestone • Glue stick
INSTRUCTIONS: Cut a 2 1/4" x 3 1/4" piece from Light Blue cardstock. Stamp with music and Light Blue ink. Tear a piece of Blue tissue and glue to card. Stamp with script and Medium Blue ink. Stamp figure in Dark Blue ink. Glue star sequin to card. Cut a 2 1/2" x 3 1/2" piece from Dark Blue cardstock. Glue layers together.

Editions and Series

An **EDITION** refers to a group of cards that are virtually identical, with the same backgrounds, focal points and embellishments arranged in the same way. These are usually numbered as one of the total number, so the first one of the edition of 100 would be 1 of 100 or 1/100.

A **SERIES** refers to a set of cards that have the same theme or unifying factor, but look different. They usually have an indicator of the name of the series included on the back. These cards are from a Shades of Green series.

Shades of Green Cards

MATERIALS: Cardstock (Dark Green, White) • Assorted rubber stamps • Dye inkpads (Light Green, Medium Green, Dark Green) • Green postage stamp • Glue stick
INSTRUCTIONS: Cut White cardstock 2 1/4" x 3 1/4" • FOR GREEN: Apply Light Green ink directly to paper, creating blotchy background. Stamp fern leaves and Chinese character in Medium Green, and butterfly and text in Dark Green. Apply postage stamp. * FOR VERDI: Stamp music in Light Green, large face in Medium Green, and text, small face and leaf in Dark Green. • FOR ALL: Cut a piece of Dark. Green cardstock 2 1/2" x 3 1/2". Glue layers together.

Metal Flashing

Flashing can usually be found in the roofing section of any hardware store.

To avoid sharp edges, cut with dull scissors rather than tin snips. Be sure to round your corners to smooth sharp points.

1. Trace around blank card with Sharpie.

2. Cut cards from flashing with dull scissors.

Fabric on Trading Cards

Printing on Muslin

1. Peel paper backing from Steam-A-Seam II.

2. Press to muslin.

3. Run backed muslin through inkjet printer.

If you've ever wanted to dip your toe in the fabric pool, ATCs are the perfect size for testing the waters. It only takes a few scraps to get started, and you don't even have to sew if you don't want to!

Buttons & Lace No-Sew Card
MATERIALS: Vintage Ephemera image • Cardstock • Floral fabric scrap • Muslin • Lace scrap • 3 small buttons • *DMC* Pearl cotton • Iron • Computer and inkjet printer • Steam-A-Seam II • Tacky glue

INSTRUCTIONS:
Cut a 2½" x 3½" piece from cardstock and Steam-A-Seam. Peel paper off one side of Steam-A-Seam, and press to wrong side of fabric. Peel off protective paper, cover with cardstock, and press to fuse. Trim excess fabric. Following directions at left, print image on muslin. Cut out and fray edges. Fuse to card. Glue lace scrap to card with Tacky Glue. Tie pearl cotton through buttons. Glue buttons to card.

Oh, Baby!
MATERIALS: Vintage Ephemera image • Cardstock • Striped fabric scraps • Muslin • Contrasting thread • 3 small safety pins • Iron • Computer and inkjet printer • Sewing machine • Steam-A-Seam II • Glue stick

INSTRUCTIONS:
Cut two 2½" x 3½" pieces from cardstock, and one from Steam-A-Seam. Peel paper off one side of Steam-A-Seam, and press to wrong side of fabric. Peel off protective paper, cover with cardstock, and press to fuse. Trim excess fabric. Following directions at left, print image and text on muslin. Trim, position on card, and fuse with iron. Stitch around all elements several times with contrasting thread. Slide 3 safety pins through fabric layer and close. Glue remaining cardstock piece to back of card to cover stitching.

Helpful Hints

When choosing fabrics for ATCs, look for prints that are small in scale. Calicos from the quilting section of most fabric stores often offer prints and plaids that look good when cut into small pieces.

Steam-A-Seam II is a fusible product that temporarily adheres pieces together. Iron to permanently bond them. It can be stitched without gumming up your sewing machine with adhesive, which is a real plus. You'll find this in the quilting section of most fabric stores.

Raid the sewing section of any craft store for embellishments. Small safety pins, buttons, pins and needles all look great attached to fabric cards.

Working with Fabric

1. Cut a 2¹/₂" x 3¹/₂" piece from Steam-A-Seam II.

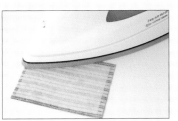

2. Peel off backing and press to fabric.

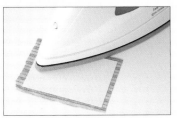

3. Peel off paper and press to cardstock.

4. Trim to size and decorate.

5. Stitch, if desired.

6. To cover stitching, glue cardstock to back of card.

Color themes are very popular in organized ATC swaps. These cards were all made with tight, monochromatic color palettes, which helps unify the diverse elements.

Fly
MATERIALS:
World Stamps paper • Black bottle caps • Vintage Children stickers • Dark Brown cardstock • Postage stamp • White mulberry paper • *Stamp Camp* word stamp • Black dye ink • Foam tape • Glue stick

INSTRUCTIONS:
Cut a 2¹/₄" x 3¹/₄" piece from World Stamps. Cut a 2¹/₂" x 3¹/₂" piece from cardstock. Glue pieces together. Tear a piece of mulberry paper, glue to card. Stamp word. Glue stamp to card. Flatten bottle cap and attach with foam tape. Adhere sticker to cap.

Cigar Store Indian
MATERIALS:
Ivory cardstock • Sheet music • Cigar band • Rubber stamps (*Bella Rosa* face; *Stamp Out Cute* American Indian) • Black dye inkpad • Corner rounder • Glue stick

INSTRUCTIONS:
Cut a 2¹/₂" x 3¹/₂" piece from cardstock. Glue sheet music to cardstock and trim. Round corners of card. Stamp face and postage on cardstock and cut out. Glue cigar band and stamped images to card.

Really Red
MATERIALS:
Cardstock (Dark Red, Light Red) • Red velour paper • Chinese Luck punch • Chinese text stamp • Red dye ink • Red mylar • Glue stick

INSTRUCTIONS:
Cut a 2¹/₄" x 3¹/₄" piece from Light Red cardstock. Stamp with Chinese text using Red dye ink. Tear a corner piece from Red velour paper. Punch with Chinese Luck, adhere Red mylar behind punch, and glue to stamped piece. Cut a 2¹/₂" x 3 ¹/₂" piece from Dark Red cardstock. Glue stamped piece to background.

Beauty
MATERIALS:
Black cardstock • Gibson Girl print • *Viva Las Vegas* face stamp • Round tag • Star-shaped brad • Black mulberry paper • Word stamp • White pigment ink • Black dye ink • Glue stick

INSTRUCTIONS:
Cut a 2¹/₄" x 3¹/₄" piece from Gibson Girl print. Tear a piece of mulberry paper, stamp word, and glue to card. Stamp face on tag and attach to card with brad. Cut a 2¹/₂" x 3¹/₂" piece from cardstock. Glue layers together.

Folded Pocket Book

This simple folded book has eight pockets sized to hold ATCs. Display your favorites with pride!

The cards displayed in our book are Designer Trading Cards by Design Originals.

Mail Art Folded Book

MATERIALS:
Journaling paper • Button snaps • Small tag • Word stamps • Brown dye inkpad • *ColorBox* Burnt Sienna chalk inkpad • Two sheets Tan 8½" x 11" paper • Hemp cord • String • Glue stick

INSTRUCTIONS:
Fold Tan paper as shown in diagram below to create two sets of pockets.

Cut cover from Journaling paper, using diagram below as guide. Fold as shown to create cover. Age edges of cover and tag with Burnt Sienna. Stamp words on tag. Attach button snaps to cover following manufacturer's directions. Wrap hemp cord around button snaps, and attach tag with string to right button. Open cover, apply a fine line of glue to spine of each set of pockets, and place against spine of cover. Close book and let dry.

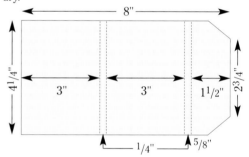

Outside Cover

Cut, tear and fold covers. Add Velcro and card where shown.

Folding the Inside Pockets

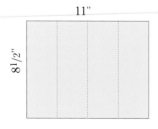

1. Fold into 4 panels of 2¾" each.

2. Fold in each edge ⅝".

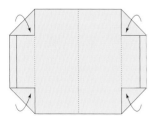

3. Fold each corner in 2⅛".

4. Fold in 2⅛" on both sides. Turn over.

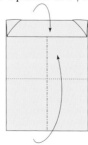

5. Turn down top ¹¹⁄₁₆". Fold bottom edge up at center.

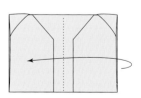

6. Fit bottom corners into pocket corners at top. Fold at center to make book. Turn over. Creates 4 pages.

Accordion Foldout Book

Corner punches designed to hold photos in place can do double duty for trading card collectors. This easy book will hold eight trading cards.

The cards displayed in our book are Designer Trading Cards by Design Originals.

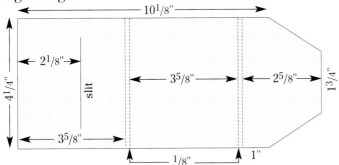

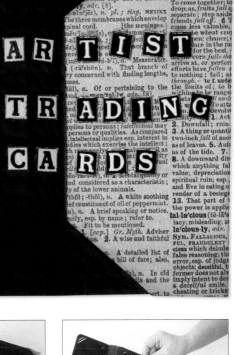

Black ATC Book

MATERIALS: Dictionary paper • Letter Squares stickers • Black cardstock • Photo corner punch • *ColorBox* Amber Clay chalk inkpad • Glue stick

INSTRUCTIONS:

Cut a strip of Black cardstock and fold according to diagram. Cover flap and half of back cover with Dictionary paper. Angle cut corners on front flap and cut a slit in front cover. Cut two strips of cardstock 4" x 12". Score every 3¹/₄". Fold on score lines into accordions. Use punch on all corners to create slits for holding cards. Glue into cover, overlapping excess flaps.

1. Accordion fold the paper.

2. Punch the corners.

3. Glue the pages to the inside of the cover.

Pockets for Cards

Pattern for Heart Pocket

Darling Love
MATERIALS:
Pink Words stickers • Lavender cardstock • Vintage photo • Melanie Sage script stamp • Purple dye ink • *ColorBox* Wisteria chalk inkpad • Foam tape • Glue stick

INSTRUCTIONS:
Cut a 2¹/₂" x 3¹/₂" piece from cardstock. Glue vintage image to cardstock and trim to size. Trace heart pocket pattern onto cardstock and cut out. Stamp with script. Fold pocket, glue, and age edges with Wisteria inkpad. Age edges of stickers and attach to pocket with foam tape. Slide card into pocket.

Pattern for Scoop Pocket

I love making trading cards that have hidden treasures. These pocket cards allow a little extra working space, and a place to hide surprises.

Library Dreams
MATERIALS:
Lock & Key paper • Library card • Date stamp • Old key • Small tag • Word stamp • White mulberry paper • String • *ColorBox* Amber Clay chalk inkpad • Black dye inkpad • Glue stick

INSTRUCTIONS:
Cut a 2¹/₂" x 3¹/₂" piece library card. Age with Amber Clay and stamp with dates. • Trace pocket pattern onto Lock & Key. Cut out, fold and glue tabs to back of pocket. Age pocket and tag with Amber Clay. Stamp word onto tag. Tie to key with string. Tear piece of mulberry paper and glue to pocket. Glue key to pocket.

You Are Just Jealous
MATERIALS:
Linen Small Floral paper • *Ink & the Dog* Eclectic stamps • *ColorBox* Rouge chalk inkpad • Buttons • String • Black dye inkpad • Manila tag • Colored pencils • Glue stick

INSTRUCTIONS:
Cut tag down to 3¹/₂" tall. Age with Rouge. Stamp face with Black ink and tint with colored pencils. Trace pocket pattern onto Small Floral and cut out. Cover back with Small Floral. Fold, glue and age with Rouge. Stamp words with Black ink. Tie string through buttons and glue to tag and pocket.

Playing Cards

An easy way to get started with ATCs without doing any cutting is to start with a deck of old, worn playing cards.

Summertime Blues

MATERIALS:
White cardstock • Playing cards • Assorted Blue postage stamps • Rhinestones • Bottle cap • Fibers • Blue Chinese coin • Silk flower petal • Rubber Stamps (Postal cancellation, Chinese character, *Diffusion* Face, *Bella Rosa* Geisha) • Star beads • Glitter glue (Silver, Iridescent) • Blue glaze • Blue Lumiere • Inkpads (Silver, Dark Blue, Black, Purple) • Silver embossing powder • Gesso • Light Blue acrylic • Sponge • Sanding block • Glue stick

INSTRUCTIONS:
Lightly sand front faces of all four cards.
For Ace Dinah: Lightly brush card with glaze and Lumiere. While still wet, lay fibers into paints. Let dry. Glue postage stamp, bottle cap and rhinestones to card. Edge with Silver glitter glue.
For #2 Geisha: Lightly brush card with glaze and Lumiere. Let dry. Stamp geisha image in Silver ink and emboss. Let dry. Stamp again, not aligning with first stamp, with Black ink. Stamp Chinese character with Dark Blue ink. Glue coin and flower petal to card.
For #3 Moon: Sponge Light Blue acrylic and gesso onto card. Let dry. Stamp face on cardstock. Glue to card. Glue star beads to card. Brush card with iridescent glitter glue.
For #4 Travel: Stamp card randomly with postage cancellations. Glue postage stamps to card. Stamp again with cancellations.

Helpful Hint

If playing cards have a plastic coating on them, rough up the surface a bit with sandpaper or a sanding block. They'll accept glue and ink better.

Wrapping With Wire

A little bit of wire adds some fun to cards that would be plain and blocky without it. The trick is to wrap the wire before mounting the card on its background, creating a clean finish.

Wire Wrapped Cards

MATERIALS:
Dark Brown Cardstock • Off-White corrugated paper • Mulberry paper or tissue • Vintage image • Wire • Seed beads (optional) • Word or character stamps • Dye inkpad • Glue stick

INSTRUCTIONS:
Cut a 2¼" x 3¼" piece from corrugated paper. Tear a piece of mulberry paper or tissue smaller than corrugated paper, but larger than image. Glue to corrugated paper. Glue image to card. Starting at back, wrap with wire several times. Twist wire at back to hold in place. Cut a 2½" x 3½" piece of Dark Brown cardstock. Glue card to background. Stamp word or character on card.

Puzzled Curiosity

MATERIALS:

Games paper • Toy Blocks cutable strip • *Ink & the Dog* Eclectic stamps • Print of vintage photo • Ivory cardstock • Puzzle pieces • String • Small tag • *ColorBox* chalk inkpad (Wisteria, Chestnut Roan) • Brown dye inkpad • Glue stick

INSTRUCTIONS:

Trace pattern onto Games paper and cut out. Fold as indicated. Age edges of interior and tag with Wisteria, and exterior and puzzle pieces with Chestnut Roan. Stamp on tag with Brown dye ink and thread with string. Mount photo on Ivory cardstock and trim. Glue to center of interior. Cut tickets from Toy Blocks strip and glue around photo. Stamp words and clocks around photo. Interlock puzzle pieces and glue the far edges of each side to front of card, centering over opening. Slide tag over one side of puzzle piece.

One Penny for Your Thoughts

MATERIALS:

Lavender cardstock • *Ink & the Dog* stamps • Purple silk ribbon • *ColorBox* chalk inkpads (Wisteria, Peony) • Dried flowers • White mulberry paper • Penny • E6000 • Glue stick

INSTRUCTIONS:

Trace pattern onto cardstock and cut out. Fold as indicated. Age edges of exterior with Wisteria, and interior with Peony. Tear a piece of mulberry paper and glue to interior of card. Stamp words with Wisteria. Stamp girl and ruler on front of folded card with Wisteria. Glue penny and dried flowers to interior of card. Glue ribbon to back of card, wrap around to front and tie in bow.

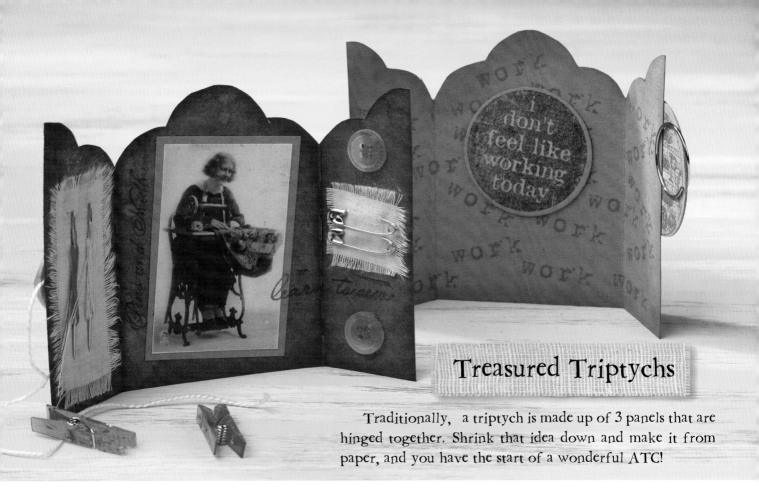

Treasured Triptychs

Traditionally, a triptych is made up of 3 panels that are hinged together. Shrink that idea down and make it from paper, and you have the start of a wonderful ATC!

Learn To Sew

MATERIALS:
Rulers paper • *ColorBox* Chestnut Roan chalk inkpad • *Ink & the Dog* Buttons stamps • Brown dye inkpad • Print of vintage photo • Tan cardstock • Muslin scraps • Needles • Small safety pins • Buttons (2 small, 1 large) • 2 tiny Gold brads • *DMC* Ivory pearl cotton • Thread (Red, Yellow) • E6000 • Glue stick

INSTRUCTIONS:
Trace pattern onto Rulers paper and cut out. Fold as indicated. Age edges of interior and exterior with Chestnut Roan. Attach large button to front of card with brads. Attach pearl cotton to button with Slip Knot. Mount photo on Tan cardstock and trim. Glue to center of interior. Tear pieces of muslin smaller than side panels of card and slide needles through one and safety pins through a second. Glue to side panels. Glue buttons to card. Wrap needles with colored thread. Stamp words on either side of photo with Brown dye ink.

Don't Feel Like Working

MATERIALS:
Kraft cardstock • *Ink & the Dog* stamps • *ColorBox* Burnt Sienna chalk inkpad • Brown dye inkpad • Spiral paper clip • Unprinted milk caps • Glue stick

INSTRUCTIONS:
Trace pattern onto cardstock and cut out. Fold as indicated. Age edges of interior and exterior with Burnt Sienna. Stamp onto milk caps with Brown dye ink. Let dry completely. Stamp numbers onto exterior, and "Work" onto interior. Glue milk caps to one side of front and center of interior. Attach spiral clip to exterior cap.

Interlocking Folds

These cards look complete when they're closed, but the real fun lies inside, behind the interlocking pieces.

Road Trip
MATERIALS:
Papers: Linen Stripe, Road Trip • Black and White Bottle caps • Road Trip stickers • Ivory cardstock • Print of vintage travel photo • Alphabet stamps • Pigment inkpads (Black, White) • Glue stick

INSTRUCTIONS:
Cut a Black piece and a White piece from Linen Stripe, and a piece of Road Trip Black slightly larger than pattern. Glue Black and White together, and then glue to Road Trip, back to back. Let dry. Trace pattern onto glued paper and cut out. Fold as indicated. Stamp words on tabs. Flatten bottle caps, decorate with stickers, and glue to front. Mat photo on Ivory cardstock and glue to center of interior. Attach stickers to interior flaps.

Easy Cards

Have fun! Create small Trading Cards to test new ink colors, rubber stamps and images.

Yellow Patchwork
MATERIALS:
Bright Yellow cardstock • Assorted rubber stamps (*Bella Rosa, Stamp Out Cute*) • Inkpads (Rust chalk, Gold pigment) • Corner rounder

INSTRUCTIONS:
Cut a 2 1/2" x 3 1/2" piece from cardstock. Stamp images in Rust ink to create patchwork background. Stamp 1 small image in Gold ink.

Make a card for every season and for every reason. You will love experimenting with fun ideas.

And your friends will love receiving surprise cards in the mail all year long!

Stitch In Time

MATERIALS:

Papers: Coffee Stripe, Coffee Floral, TeaDye Script • Print of vintage photo • 7 small buttons • *DMC* Brown pearl cotton • Alphabet stamps • Brown dye inkpad • *ColorBox* Chestnut Roan chalk inkpad • Glue stick

INSTRUCTIONS:

Cut a piece of Coffee Stripe and Coffee Floral slightly larger than pattern. Glue together, back to back. Let dry. Trace pattern onto glued paper and cut out. Fold as indicated. Age edges with Chestnut Roan. Mount photo onto TeaDye Script and trim. Glue to center of interior. Stamp text on either side of photo. Glue buttons in place. Wrap card with pearl cotton and tie in knot. Tie pearl cotton through four buttons and glue to front tabs.

Autumn Leaf

MATERIALS:

Autumn Leaves paper • Gold vellum • Silk leaf • Chinese character stamp • Brown pigment ink • Glue stick

INSTRUCTIONS:

Cut a 2¹/₂" x 3¹/₂" piece from Leaves paper. Tear a strip of vellum and glue to card. Glue leaf over vellum. Stamp character with Brown ink.

Happy Halloween

by Michele Charles

MATERIALS:

Papers: Rust Linen, Dictionary, Halloween • Cream cardstock • *Dymo* labeler • *Ranger* Black Soot Distress ink • *ColorBox* Sepia Black ink • Adhesive

INSTRUCTIONS:

Cut a 2¹/₂" x 3¹/₂" piece from Rust paper. Tear Dictionary paper and glue to card. Cut images from Halloween paper and glue to card. Shadow images with Sepia Black. Rub Black Soot on edges of card. Thread cream cardstock thru Dymo. Type out words. Cut strips. Highlight words with Black Soot. Glue to card.

Paint Chip Samples

One of my favorite free art materials is paint sample cards. Perhaps you have some leftover from your last home painting venture. These come in every size, shape and color combination, and are the ideal size for smaller projects like ATCs.

Field of Butterflies
MATERIALS: Paint sample card • *Rubber Stampede* (Wild Grass, Monte Casino Spring, Butterfly) • Dye inkpads (Light Brown, Dark Brown)
INSTRUCTIONS: Cut paint sample card using instructions below. Stamp dried grass with Light Brown, and flowers and butterfly with Dark Brown. If desired, cover back of card with paper or cardstock.

Daisy in Bamboo
MATERIALS: Paint sample card • Ivory cardstock • Asian text paper • Dried daisy • Corner rounder punch • Glue stick
INSTRUCTIONS: Cut a 2 1/2" x 3 1/2" piece from cardstock. Glue Asian text to cardstock. Cut paint sample card in strips of varying widths. Glue strips onto card. Trim ends to card height. Round the corners. Glue daisy to card.

Ride 'em Cowgirl
MATERIALS: Paint sample card • Print of cowgirl image • Postage stamp • Glue stick
INSTRUCTIONS: Cut a 2 1/2" x 3 1/2" piece from paint sample card. Cut around outline of cowgirl. Glue to card. Glue postage stamp to card, sliding corner behind cowgirl's head. If desired, cover back of card with paper or cardstock.

1. Make a diagonal cut across paint chip to define long edge.

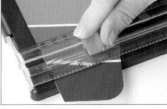

2. Square up one side from diagonal cut.

3. Cut 2 1/2" wide.

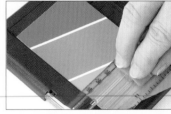

4. Cut 3 1/2" high.

Helpful Hint

You can remove printed words and numbers from most paint samples with a White plastic eraser. It takes a little elbow grease, but it's worth it!

ATCs and ACEOs

The creators of artist trading cards stipulated that they should be traded between artists, and never sold. With the rise in popularity of ATC trading, there is a growing interest in selling and purchasing cards. Trading cards that are made for sale are called ACEOs: Artist Cards, Editions and Originals.